nutrition

by Paul Thompson

A FIRST BOOK

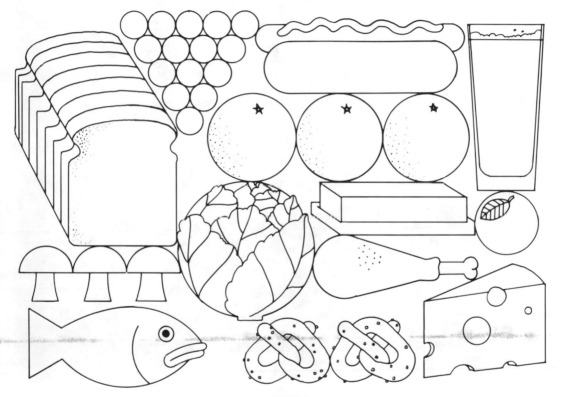

A GROLIER COMPANY

FRANKLIN WATTS

New York | London | Toronto | Sydney | 1981

TO GWENDOLYN ANNE

The author would like to thank Judith Marlett, Assistant Professor of Nutritional Sciences at the University of Wisconsin-Madison, for reading the manuscript of this book and offering criticisms and suggestions. He would also like to thank Carol Allen, assistant scientist in cell biology at the University of Wisconsin-Madison, for reading Chapter Two of the manuscript. The author, however, must accept responsibility for any errors of fact or interpretation in the book.

Photographs courtesy of: World Health Organization: pp. 3, 53; USDA Photo: pp. 8, 23, 32, 40; Grant Heilman: p. 9; The Bettmann Archive: p. 15; Linda Moore/Rainbow: p. 16; Rogers/Monkmeyer Press Photo Service: p. 56.

Library of Congress Cataloging in Publication Data

Thompson, Paul, 1938–
Nutrition.

(A First book)
Bibliography: p.
Includes index.
Summary: Discusses carbohydrates, fats, proteins, vitamins, minerals, and how the body uses them; diet; and food additives.
1. Nutrition—Juvenile literature.
[1. Nutrition]   I. Title.
TX355.T455   641.1   81–7413
ISBN 0–531–04328–2   AACR2

CONTENTS

NUTRITION

FOOD AND PEOPLE

Fossil remains show that our ancestors roamed the warmer parts of Africa, Asia, and Europe more than a million years ago.

They were hunters and gatherers, living off the wild land. Even today, a few people in remote parts of the world follow this way of life. From them we can learn something of how our distant ancestors lived.

They moved about in small groups, a few families in each band. At times, several groups might come together to hold ceremonies, visit, and gossip. But it was hard to provide food for a large gathering for more than a few weeks or months, and these gatherings always broke up into smaller roving groups again. However, in places where the food supply was particularly abundant, more settled communities sometimes developed.

(1)

FROM BERRIES
TO BEETLES

To most of us, nature is a mysterious blur of green that we learn about by reading. Early people "read" nature directly, paying keen attention to every detail. Their lives depended on it. They had names for and knew the uses of dozens of plants and animals. From the tracks of an antelope, a hunter could tell its sex, size, age, state of health, and how long it had been since the animal passed that way.

Much of their food came from fruits, nuts, and berries. Our ancestors also made good use of roots, leafy greens, seed pods, grass seeds, and mushrooms. Women, who usually had children to nurse, could not easily take part in hunting. But they did much of the other food gathering.

The men hunted a wide variety of animals with simple but effective weapons. A thrown pebble or stick could knock down birds and small animals. These creatures could also be caught in snares. Stone-tipped spears could kill larger animals. (Bows and arrows are a fairly recent invention in the history of the world.) It was also quite easy to scavenge. A lion that had killed its prey and eaten enough to take the edge off its hunger, could be driven away by shouts. This left the half-eaten prey for the men.

COOKING

The world was a very large place for these ancestors of ours. There were only a few hundred thousand people on earth. A

This early rock painting from a town in the Sahara Desert shows people hunting antelope and giraffe with bows and arrows and with spears.

(2)

visitor from space would have been much more likely to notice the huge herds of grazing animals or the flocks of birds than the occasional band of humans.

But a half-million or more years ago, something new happened. Here and there across the landscape, a thread of smoke rose in the air. It marked a campsite where food was being cooked.

Nobody knows how humans came to use fire for cooking. Perhaps they first discovered the joy of cooking by tasting animals killed in grass fires. Eventually, they learned to make their own fires. Women, along with caring for the children, tended the fire and did much of the cooking.

The use of fire was a major change in human life. Cooking softens tough foods and makes them easier to eat. It also makes many foods, such as meat and seed grains, more digestible and nourishing.

Early people had no cooking pots, but this did not stop them. Much of their food was roasted over the fire in the same way we grill hamburgers and steaks. Another technique, still used today in many places, is to bury the food in hot coals or sand. In his book, *Animate Creation*, the English writer J. G. Wood described how Africans a century ago cooked one delicacy, elephant's foot:

> *This part of the animal is cooked by being laid in a hole in the earth, over which a large fire has been suffered to burn itself out, and then covered with the hot earth. Another fire is built on the spot, and permitted to burn itself out as before, and when the place is thoroughly cool, the food is properly cooked. The flesh of the boiled foot is quite soft . . . and is so tender that it can be scooped away with a spoon.*

FROM HUNTING
TO FARMING

Our early ancestors lived a vigorous life. But it may not have been as hard as we used to imagine. Scientists who have gone and lived among hunting and gathering people today have found that nature can be very generous. Quite often, enough food for several days can be gathered in a few hours. In addition, because our ancestors had such a varied diet, famines were rare, for there was always some kind of food at hand.

A great change occurred, however, some 10,000 years ago. We don't know why it came. It took place in several parts of the world. In each region the change took centuries, but this is just an instant compared to the total amount of time people have been on earth.

Scientists and historians call it the agricultural revolution. One of the places it happened was in the Middle East. People learned to plant seeds and harvest the plants that grew. Among these were wild grasses that became our modern wheats. People also tamed and put animals such as dogs, sheep, and cattle to use. The farming revolution gave them greater control over their food supply.

Elsewhere in the world other people were learning to domesticate plants and animals. To name just a few: soybeans and pigs in China; rice and chickens in Southeast Asia; alfalfa and horses in Central Asia; watermelons and donkeys in Africa; oats and cattle in Europe; potatoes and llamas in South America; and maize (corn) and turkeys in North America.

THE RISE OF CITIES

Farming encouraged the growth of settled communities, for a farmer cannot pick up his fields and trot off with them the way a hunter can with his bow and spear.

It also encouraged people to cooperate and plan ahead. Building irrigation ditches, for example, could take years of work by a community. A more settled life led to larger families, so the world's population began to rise slowly. With more people, there was a need for government, and also, an increase in trade.

Change stimulated more change. Pottery was invented, metals were put to use in tools and weapons, people began using metal coins instead of bartering goods, and the need for records in farming, trade, and government led to the invention of writing and mathematics. While most towns remained small, some grew into cities that became centers of government, trade, religion, and learning.

In many ways, life for the common person was harder in the new age. Most men and women labored from dawn to dusk in the fields. Much of their produce was taken by the government through taxes or by wealthy landlords. The choice of food was narrowed tremendously. The cereal grains and a few other foods like milk and olives became the foundation of life. A couple of bad crop years could mean famine. The frequent wars between neighboring kingdoms often brought famine, too, as armies destroyed crops and irrigation works.

THE MODERN AGE

Despite wars, famine, and disease epidemics, the world's population slowly grew. There were perhaps 300 million men, women, and children in the world in the year 1 A.D. By 1750, that figure had grown to some 800 million.

During all those long centuries, the average person still labored in the fields. But in the last two centuries, a series of new "revolutions" have greatly changed the life of the common person.

Starting in England, the Industrial Revolution began replacing manual labor and animal power with machinery. This made people much more productive. By making it possible for men and women to produce more goods and services with less labor, general prosperity was increased.

The Industrial Revolution spread to the rest of Western Europe and to North America. In the United States and Canada, a new kind of agriculture was born. The farmer turned his horse or mule out to pasture and bought a tractor. Scientists from universities and government gave him better fertilizers, new pesticides to control insects and weeds, and improved varieties of plants and animals.

In 1820, the average American farmer could produce enough food to feed himself and three other people. By 1945, he could feed himself and fourteen other people, while today he can feed himself and forty-six other people.

Since fewer people are needed to produce our food, many men and women have moved to the cities to work in factories and offices. Today, the United States, Canada, and the countries of Western Europe are urban nations, with most people living in towns and cities.

Food handling has been revolutionized, too. Crops are taken to market by truck, rail, and ship. They are processed in factories and packaged for sale in the supermarket. We have a much greater choice of foods than our ancestors did. Fruits and vegetables are available year-round.

This new form of agri-business, as the food production system is sometimes called, has become widespread in the wealthier countries of the world. But in the poorer nations, many people still toil on the land, raising food the same way they have for centuries.

The changes of the last two centuries have triggered a

*The use of machinery like this
lettuce harvester has greatly
increased agricultural production
in the industrialized nations.*

*These tomatoes are growing in a solution of water
and chemical fertilizers, without soil.
Innovations such as this are needed if food production
is to keep pace with the world's expanding population.*

"population explosion." The world's population is now more than 4,000 million people. It is expected to reach 6,000 million by the year 2000. Agriculture has barely kept up with the increasing number of mouths to feed. It is said that one-third of the world's people either do not get enough to eat or do not get enough of the right kinds of food for good health. This is the greatest challenge of *nutrition*. But life in nations like our own also has nutritional challenges.

JAWS: WHY WE MUST EAT

In fairy tales, magical transformations take place. People are changed into frogs, trees, swans—and back again. A similar "magical" transformation happens each time you sit down at the dinner table.

Down your throat go chicken, green beans, and potatoes. Then, as you sit back feeling good, your body starts changing the chicken and vegetables into human tissue, bone, and blood.

It took scientists hundreds of years to discover how one kind of living thing can be changed into another kind of living thing. Even now, we don't know all the answers. But we have learned that the trick is possible only because all living creatures are made up basically of the same chemical building blocks.

These same building blocks can make a chicken, a person, a beetle, or a carrot. When you eat a meal, your body breaks down the meat and vegetables into their basic building blocks and then rebuilds them into *you*.

(11)

WE'RE ALL
CARBON COPIES

Many of the chemical ingredients of life have been discovered by scientists. The most important ones include the sugars that make up the food substances called *carbohydrates*, the *fatty acids* that make up *fats* and *oils*, and the *amino acids* that link together to form *proteins*. We will be discussing these building blocks later on. But all of them include one key substance: the black stuff you scrape off burnt toast.

For the black stuff is mostly *carbon*, and without it none of us would be around. There would not be any microbes, trees, parrots, or people. Carbon is the starting point of life.

Carbon is one of the more than 100 basic elements in the universe. The "lead" in a pencil is a form of pure carbon called graphite. Diamond is another form of pure carbon. Charcoal is also mostly carbon.

Carbon is special among the elements because the carbon atom is handier than most at linking up with other atoms, especially other carbon atoms. At the same time, those carbon atoms can grab onto atoms of other elements like oxygen and hydrogen. In this way, carbon atoms can build up the large complicated *molecules* (clusters of atoms) found in living things.

Without the assistance of carbon, most other elements can form only simple molecules. These molecules are rather limited in what they can do. Take water, for example, whose molecule is made up of two hydrogen atoms and one oxygen atom. Water can flow, freeze, and evaporate—but not much else. But with the large, complicated molecules carbon makes possible, you wind up with creatures that can dance, sing, dream, build space ships, kill each other in wars, and fall in love.

ONE REASON
WHY WE EAT—
FOR GROWTH

Take a good look at your hand. Bones give it strength. Muscles and tendons allow you to grasp objects. Skin encloses and protects. Fingernails give extra protection to the tips of your fingers. The entire structure is built out of carbon molecules, water, and *minerals*.

When you were a newborn infant, your hand was tiny and hardly able to grasp your parent's finger. Now your hand is able to grasp a softball or play the piano. Obviously, to grow to your present size, you needed a supply of carbon-containing molecules and other materials to add to those already in your body. That's one important purpose of eating—to provide you with materials for growth.

Even after you reach your full size, some parts of your body will not stop "growing." Old cells die, and their materials get broken down and excreted from your body. You will always need a fresh supply of carbon building materials to provide replacement cells and maintain your body.

WHERE DO WE
GET OUR ENERGY?

Flex your fingers. Clench your fist. Where does the energy to do that come from? Press your hand against your cheek. Feel the warmth of your skin. Where does that heat come from?

Over two centuries ago, scientists were curious about body motion and heat. The warmth of the body reminded them of the heat given off by flames. Could life be something like a flame, in which fuel was burned and energy given off?

A French scientist, Antoine Lavoisier, studied how candles burn. Candle wax, manufactured from substances like animal fats, is made up of carbon molecules. Lavoisier found that in the flame of a candle, carbon molecules are joining with oxygen atoms from the air. This process produces heat and light. We call it burning. As a waste product, the flame gives off *carbon dioxide*, an invisible gas produced by the union of carbon and oxygen.

The importance of oxygen to burning was shown by placing a lit candle inside a closed jar. When the oxygen in the jar was all used up, the candle went out.

Lavoisier also studied guinea pigs and humans. He found fascinating similarities between living creatures and the candle. For one thing, guinea pigs and humans use oxygen from the air. They breathe out carbon dioxide. When a guinea pig was placed inside a closed jar, it lived only as long as there was oxygen in the jar. When the oxygen was used up by the animal's breathing, it died.

Lavoisier decided that in some way living creatures "burn" carbon to produce the energy they need. This was only half right. It is true that the cells combine oxygen with carbon molecules and give off carbon dioxide as a waste product. This does release energy. But it is done in a series of chemical steps that has little resemblance to the flame of a candle. The energy is used for various cell activities. Only after the energy has done its work does it become heat and escape from the body.

WE NEED TO RENEW
OUR FUEL SUPPLY

Since the carbon "burned" in the body is breathed out into the air as carbon dioxide, we steadily lose some of our carbon. How is this loss replaced? By eating. So besides providing material for body-building, eating supplies us with fuel.

The energy released by the union of carbon and oxygen

*The French scientist Lavoisier
conducts his famous
experiment with oxygen.*

*Regular exercise ensures that the body
will use most of the carbon "fuel"
it gets from food to produce energy.*

in the body appears in several different forms: chemical energy used in building body substances; energy of motion such as the pumping of the heart and the movement of our bodies; even electrical energy in our nerves and brain. After a while, however, just about all of the energy turns into waste heat and escapes from the body.

COUNTING CALORIES

French scientists trying to measure heat invented a unit of measure for heat called the *calorie*. The body gives off millions of calories of heat each day. It is inconvenient to use such large numbers, so scientists who study the human body use a unit of heat measurement they call the "large calorie" or "kilocalorie." This is equal to 1,000 small calories. The use of the word "calorie" in connection with nutrition means the large calorie.

A twelve-year-old boy or girl loses more than 2,000 calories (large calories) of heat each day as his or her body releases and uses energy stored in carbon molecules.

The body has some wonderful, delicate ways of adjusting energy production to meet your needs. When you sleep, only enough energy is produced to keep you breathing, to keep your heart beating, and so forth. As you wake up and get out of bed, the cells begin consuming carbon molecules at a more rapid rate. Energy production soars still higher as you get dressed, eat breakfast, and head off for school or play.

A person leading a vigorous life with plenty of exercise uses a lot more fuel and needs to eat bigger meals than a person who spends most of his or her time watching television.

We say that a slice of white bread contains enough energy locked up in its carbon molecules to yield between 60 and 65 calories of heat. A frankfurter will yield about 170 calories of heat.

(17)

But remember, the calorie is simply a unit of measurement. We often speak of food as "containing calories," but that is not really accurate. A slice of bread does not contain calories any more than it contains inches or ounces. It contains energy that can be measured in calories.

CALORIES ARE
NOT ENOUGH

If the fuel value of food were all that mattered, you could live very cheaply on just bread, or potatoes, or lard.

In the 1760s, a London doctor named William Stark was fascinated by stories of people who lived on very limited diets. He had a letter from Benjamin Franklin, for example, describing how as a young man Franklin had lived for two weeks on nothing but bread and water and had remained "stout and hearty." Dr. Stark had also heard of a lady of ninety who, it was said, lived on nothing but pure meat fat.

His mind filled with these and other stories, Dr. Stark began a search for the perfect diet. He used himself as a guinea pig.

For a month, he ate nothing but bread and water. Then bread, water, and sugar. Far from remaining stout and hearty, he got sores on the inside of his mouth. His gums swelled and bled. He had given himself scurvy, a dangerous disease that we now know is caused by a lack of vitamin C in the diet.

But Dr. Stark did not give up. He tried bread, water, and olive oil. Then bread, water, and milk. Then bread, water, and roast goose. And so on. The last diet was just bread and tea. It was the last because Dr. Stark, weakened by his experiment, died of a fever.

Dr. Stark was a courageous but foolish man. Thoughtful people had already observed that a limited diet is usually a poor one. Calories are not enough.

The body needs fuel. But it also needs materials to repair itself and grow—to build bones, muscles, and other tissue. It needs still other substances just to keep working properly. No one food can provide the body with everything it needs. The more different foods we include in our diets, the more likely we are to get everything we need.

THE FUEL FOODS: CARBOHYDRATES

Do you like jelly sandwiches? Do you think your body uses a jelly sandwich mostly for fuel, or for growth?

If you answered "fuel," you are correct.

Bread and jelly are rich in food substances called *carbohydrates,* which the body uses to produce energy. In a pinch, the body can use other food substances as fuel, but it gets energy most easily and efficiently from carbohydrates. If you tried to get along without carbohydrates, you could fall ill with a disease doctors call *ketosis*.

Fortunately, carbohydrates are among our most plentiful and cheapest of foods. There are two interesting things about carbohydrates: (1) they are produced mostly by plants and (2) the plants build them out of sugar.

In fact, every plant is a kind of sugar factory. It uses the energy of sunlight to make sugar out of water and air. This manufacturing goes on in the green parts of plants, especially the leaves. The sugar dissolves in the watery sap of the leaves and is carried to all parts of the plant to nourish the cells. Each plant cell depends upon sugar for the energy it needs to live and do its work. Sugar is the simplest kind of carbohydrate, and when we eat it our bodies use it as fuel.

NATURE'S SWEETS

Since the dawn of humanity, people have enjoyed eating the sugars produced by plants. Fruits are sweet because of the plant sugar they contain. Flowers produce sugar-rich nectar, which bees turn into honey. The sugar on our table comes from the stalks of the sugar cane or the roots of the sugar beet plant.

Just about every food we eat contains some sugar put there by nature. Food companies also use a great deal of sugar to make their products more attractive to shoppers. Soft drinks and snack foods, for example, are often loaded with sugar. Some cold cereals are coated with sugar or honey to make them more appealing to children.

None of these sweet foods is unhealthy if eaten once in a while. The problem is, however, that some people constantly snack on sugary foods. This spoils their appetites for food that contain the *vitamins* and *minerals* needed for health. It also promotes tooth decay, especially if they don't rinse their mouths or brush their teeth after snacking.

In Chapter 8, "What Is a Good Diet?," we'll talk about some nutritious substitutes for sugary snacks.

OUR DAILY BREAD

Plants produce more sugar than they need for energy. They store some of the extra sugar. In one form of storage, the plant takes molecules of sugar and links them together to form very long chains, like beads on a necklace. In this form, the sugar is called *starch*.

Like sugar, starch is a carbohydrate. Our bodies use it for fuel. We find a lot of starch in wheat, rice, corn, and other grains. Breakfast cereals made from these grains contain a lot of starch. Because baked goods are made from wheat flour, we know that bread, biscuits, and pizza crust are rich in starch. So are macaroni and spaghetti.

Root vegetables like potatoes, carrots, turnips, parsnips, and sweet potatoes are also starchy. Starchy foods such as bread and potatoes are an important part of most diets because they are low in cost, filling, and provide needed fuel for the body.

These foods usually provide more than fuel. Although they are mostly starch, they also contain some other food substances needed by the body for good nutrition and growth. Bread, for example, contains B vitamins needed for your body to work properly, iron needed by your blood, and calcium needed to make strong bones.

HOW DIGESTION WORKS

Before the body can "burn" carbohydrates, it must digest them. Let's see how this happens.

When you take a bite of bread and chew it, your teeth cut and grind the bread into small pieces. At the same time, saliva mixes with the bread. The saliva moistens the bread so it will slide easily down your throat. It also starts the digestion process.

Saliva contains a chemical substance called *salivary amylase*. Each molecule of amylase acts like a pair of chemical scissors. You will remember that starch is made up of chains of sugar molecules. When a molecule of amylase bumps into a

Bread, pasta, and grains
such as rice and oats are nutritious
sources of carbohydrates.

starch chain, it snips it apart. Then it drifts on, to do the same thing elsewhere. Meanwhile, many other amylase molecules are also busy at work breaking down starch chains.

Amylase is one of the body substances called *enzymes*. Enzymes are molecules that break down or build up materials inside the body. Many enzymes are involved in digestion. Each works much like salivary amylase, snipping apart food molecules into smaller units.

TO THE
STOMACH
AND BEYOND

While the amylase is working, the bread slips down the esophagus, into the stomach.

If you have ever had the misfortune to be sick to your stomach, you know that the material coming up has a sour taste. That is the taste of hydrochloric acid.

This acid kills most bacteria, helping to protect us from harmful disease germs in food, although some occasionally do slip through alive. The acid also halts the action of the salivary amylase. This stops starch digestion temporarily. The stomach does have enzymes that begin attacking fats and proteins in the bread, however.

The bread's next stop is the small intestine, where the starch chains run into enzymes that again start snipping the chains apart. After a while, the starch is broken down into separate molecules of sugar. These molecules are small enough to be absorbed by the walls of the small intestine. Here they enter tiny blood vessels. The blood carries molecules of sugar to every cell of the body. The cells combine the sugar with oxygen to release energy.

WHAT IS
FOOD FIBER?

There are plant carbohydrates that are made of sugar molecules but cannot be digested by the body's enzymes. These are *cellulose* and other materials that make up the fibrous or woody parts of plants.

Some animals have enzymes that can digest cellulose; this is why termites can get nourishment from wood, and cows from grass. We lack those enzymes, so the fibers pass through into the large intestine with other waste material. This *fiber,* or *roughage,* however, is important in keeping the waste bulky so the lower intestine works properly and we don't become constipated. It's important to have fiber in our diets.

Fruits, vegetables, and whole wheat bread are good sources of roughage.

SUMMING UP

In this chapter, we've talked about the carbohydrates. Although some foods, such as fruit and bread, are rich in carbohydrates, few foods contain *only* carbohydrates. Most foods also contain other food substances.

We have also seen how digestion works. The body breaks food substances down into small units. These are absorbed by the body. It can either use them as fuel or build them up into body substances. This is how food loses its identity and becomes *you.*

STORED FUEL: FATS AND OILS

Do you ever put money aside to buy something special? Plants and animals have "savings accounts," too. They have ways of storing food up in their cells for a time when it will be needed. Plants often store sugar as starch, for example. There is also a starch-like carbohydrate found in small amounts in animals, called glycogen.

Another way living things store up food is in the form of fat. In plants, fats take the form of oily liquids called vegetable oils. Some plant seeds are especially rich in oil. Does your family use vegetable oil in cooking? Check the bottle to see what kind of plant the oil came from. Oil can be obtained from soybeans, corn, peanuts, and olives.

In animals, fat is usually solid rather than liquid. It is stored in special cells crammed with fat. Under our skins, for example, we have a layer of fat cells. This layer helps to insulate us against the cold, and provides a cushion to protect us from bumps. It is also a food "savings account." When we take in more food—whether carbohydrates, fats, or proteins—than our body can use, the extra food is converted into fat.

This is done by rearranging the atoms in the molecules to make new molecules called *fatty acids*. Then the fatty acids are hooked up together to make oil or fat. When other fuels are in short supply, the fat is "burned" instead, to provide energy. Fats are a very concentrated source of energy. When combined with oxygen in the cell, they yield twice the energy released by the same amount of carbohydrates.

HOW DOES
THE BODY
DIGEST FAT?

The fat in our food must be digested before it can be used by the body. It passes through the upper part of the digestive tract with little change. That is why a meal rich in fat leaves you feeling full longer than does a meal rich in carbohydrates. But in the small intestine, the fat is hit with a double whammy: bile and enzymes.

Bile is a yellowish-orange liquid that is nature's own miracle detergent. Just as your dishwashing detergent lifts grease from pots and plates, and floats it off in the water as fine particles, so bile attacks clumps of fat and breaks them down into smaller particles. These particles can then be acted upon by enzymes called lipases. They split up the fat molecules into free fatty acids.

The small intestine absorbs the fatty acids. They are carried by the blood to various parts of the body. Some of the fat is used for energy by the cells. The rest is stored in the fat cells and used later.

(27)

WHY FAT IS USEFUL

Besides being a food storehouse, fat serves some other important purposes in the body. As mentioned before, fat under the skin helps insulate us and cushion us. Some organs are protected from shock by being enclosed in fatty tissue. Our eyes are cushioned in their sockets by fatty tissue. The liver is another organ with a cushion of fat around it. The body's cells themselves have parts made up of fat molecules.

The body can make just about all the fat molecules it needs by converting sugar or other food substances into fatty acids. However, there are two fatty acids that the body cannot manufacture; it must get these from fat in the diet. Certain fats in the diet, like the fats in milk and butter, also carry along with them vitamins the body needs for good health. So a fat-free diet would not be healthy.

HIDDEN FATS

In fact, it would be almost impossible to have a truly fat-free diet. Fats are a part of many of our foods—even foods that may not appear to contain fat. Some fats—like butter and margarine—are highly visible. But many are not. Did you know that chocolate is rich in fat? And nuts? Even if we trim off the visible fat from meat, there is fat in the whitish "marbling" in the main part of the meat. Many baked goods contain a considerable amount of fat.

Nutritionists worry that some people eat too much fat, especially in snack foods that contain few vitamins or minerals. Like sugary snacks, the fatty snacks dull the appetite without providing much in the way of nutrition except for fuel. Potato chips, made from slices of potato fried in fat, are an example of a fatty snack that provides little in the way of nutrition.

We are smart to avoid such snacks, for we will get enough fat simply from our regular meals. And people with a weight problem need to cut back on fatty foods in general, for their own fat comes from eating more fuel foods than their bodies can use up by "burning" it for energy. Eating a lot of fatty foods simply adds to the problem.

PROTEINS FOR GROWTH

Carbohydrates and fats are fuel foods. But the body needs more than energy. It needs materials to build cells and tissues. The most important building material by far is *protein*.

Nearly everything in your body is made of protein: muscles, skin, bones, hair, even your fingernails. In addition, protein performs vital jobs in body chemistry. The enzymes that digest foods, for example, are protein molecules.

The body constructs its own protein, but it needs to get the building blocks for these molecules from protein in food. If your food did not contain protein, you would eventually stop growing. Then you would begin wasting away, because your body could not repair or replace cells damaged by the wear and tear of ordinary living. This would happen even if your food contained plenty of carbohydrates, fats, and other food substances.

In fact, this kind of stunted growth and wasting away actually occurs in some unfortunate children in poor countries.

Their parents can afford only starchy foods, and can't buy meat, fish, and other foods rich in protein. Some of the children get so little protein that they waste away and die. This disease is called kwashiorkor, a name that comes from the language of Ghana in Africa.

Fortunately, kwashiorkor almost never occurs in our nation. That's because protein-rich foods are plentiful, and nearly everybody can afford to buy them.

PROTEIN
BUILDING BLOCKS

The protein in muscle is not exactly like the protein in your fingernails. There are thousands of different kinds of protein in the body, each important in its own way.

In constructing proteins, the body follows the same rule it uses in building carbohydrates and fats. It links together simple molecules to make more complicated ones. The basic building blocks of proteins are small molecules called *amino acids*. There are about twenty animo acids. They can be hooked together in many different combinations to form proteins.

Proteins in our food must be digested before the body can make use of their amino acids. The hydrochloric acid in the stomach, together with an enzyme called pepsin, breaks proteins apart into short chains. Still other enzymes continue this snipping work in the small intestine. The amino acids are absorbed there, and carried by the blood to all parts of the body.

THE ESSENTIAL
AMINO ACIDS

The cells link amino acids together to make the proteins they need. If a certain kind of amino acid is missing, the cell can

*Protein is found in a wide variety
of foods—meat, fish, poultry, and
eggs, as well as such vegetable products
as beans, peas, and peanuts.*

often manufacture it by rearranging the atoms in another amino acid. But there are some amino acids the body cannot make itself, and these must be gotten from the food we eat. These are called *essential amino acids*. There are ten of them.

Some foods, such as milk and eggs, have just about all the amino acids used by the human body. Nutritionists say that these foods provide "complete" protein. The protein is "complete" because it provides all the essential amino acids in amounts the body can use. Other foods provide some but not all of the essential amino acids. These are called "incomplete" proteins.

Protein of animal origin tends to be more "complete" than protein of plant origin. So it is wise to include some animal protein in the diet, although vegetarians can get enough of the essential amino acids by choosing their foods carefully. This task is easier if their philosophy about food allows them to eat eggs or milk.

Eggs and milk are two good sources of animal protein. Cheese, yogurt, and ice cream also contain some protein. Red meat, poultry, and fish are also rich in protein.

Foods from plants that provide a lot of protein include beans, peas, and nuts. Grains provide some protein too, although they are mostly carbohydrate.

You don't really have to worry about getting enough protein. Most of us in the United States, Canada, and Europe get enough—often more than we need.

ENTER THE VITAMINS

In the closing months of 1870, the people of Paris were starving. The German Army was camped around the French capital city, and no food was distributed to the citizens. The mothers of Paris were desperate, for their infants were dying from lack of milk.

The new science of food chemistry had shown that milk was a mixture of water, butterfat, sugars, and protein. Faced with the pleas of mothers, Paris scientists tried to produce an artificial milk by combining water, fat, sugar, and a protein material.

It did not work. The infants continued to die. A French scientist, J. B. A. Dumas, sadly concluded that scientists still lacked vital knowledge. There seemed to be something more to food than carbohydrates, fats, and proteins.

Many food scientists, proud of their achievements, failed to pay heed to the lesson of the Paris seige. In America, for example, one of the leading food chemists was advising housewives to stop buying fruit and vegetables, because sugar and flour were a much cheaper source of carbohydrates. Fortunately, most housewives ignored his advice.

How wrong he was was shown by experiments in feeding laboratory animals such as rats. Although every substance thought to be important was included in these diets, the animals became sick and died. But when very small amounts of natural foods were added to the rations, the animals thrived. What was missing from the rations that was supplied by the added bits of natural food?

THE DEFICIENCY DISEASES

Long before the food researchers started their experiments on rats, people were carrying out unintentional diet experiments on themselves.

During wars or on long voyages, for example, people deprived of fresh fruits and vegetables often developed bleeding gums. Their teeth fell out. Internal bleeding weakened them, and they often died.

The British Navy found that a daily ration of citrus juice (from lemons or limes) prevented *scurvy*, as this dread disease was called. This led American sailors to nickname the British sailors "limeys."

The Gold Rush brought 100,000 pioneers to California in 1849–1850. With fresh food in short supply, 10,000 people died of scurvy in the mining camps. Some pioneers planted lemon trees to meet the demand for citrus. Thus began California's large citrus industry.

There were other diseases that some observant doctors suspected were linked to diet. In Asia, people whose main food was rice developed an ailment called *beriberi* when they ate the new-fangled polished white rice that had had its brown coat removed. Switching back to the brown rice cured the disease.

Then there were eye disorders among poorly-nourished people in many parts of the world. These eye problems could often be cleared up by adding animal fat to the diet.

There was *rickets,* a bone-crippling disease common among children in large cities where they did not get enough sunlight and fresh foods. People soon found that rickets could be cured by administering cod-liver oil.

Many doctors in the late 1800s ignored this evidence, however. They were so taken with the new discovery that many diseases were caused by germs that they felt unknown microbes must be behind illnesses like beriberi.

But the chemists performing animal experiments found the idea of links between diet and disease very interesting. Their animal tests gave them a way to search for those links.

THE VITAMINS

In 1912, Casimir Funk, a Polish chemist working in London, put the new thinking into words. He proposed that beriberi, scurvy, and rickets were all caused by substances that were lacking in certain diets. He suggested the name of "vitamines" for these substances. The final "e" was later dropped.

Proof was already being found in the laboratories of Europe and the United States through animal feeding tests. Gradually, scientists tracked down these mysterious substances so important to health.

They discovered that a substance found in animal fats, especially in milkfat, was needed for good night vision. Its lack caused "night blindness" and certain other eye disorders.

They named this substance *vitamin A*. Vitamin A is also found in dark green and yellow vegetables.

The substance in brown rice and other whole cereal grains that prevents beriberi was called *vitamin B*. Evidence was found for *vitamin C* in fresh fruits and vegetables, the anti-scurvy vitamin. The vitamin in cod-liver oil and certain other foods that cured rickets was named *vitamin D*.

But this system of naming began to break down as scientists learned more. Vitamin B turned out to be just one of a whole group of vitamins often found together. They were labeled B_1, B_2, etc. Then, as the vitamins were isolated in pure form and given chemical names, many scientists began using those names. Vitamin C is also called ascorbic acid, for example.

Today, a vitamin is usually known by more than one name. Scientists are not confused by this, but the rest of us often are.

Chemists have found that vitamins are small molecules containing carbon. They are found only in tiny amounts in our food, but are essential to our health.

Why does the body need vitamins? Researchers have found that many vitamins form part of key enzymes. Vitamin D, on the other hand, serves as a chemical messenger in the body to stimulate it to absorb calcium from the diet. Without it, calcium is not properly absorbed and rickets develops.

Interestingly, the body itself manufactures vitamin D when exposed to sunlight. When we don't get enough sunshine, then we must get vitamin D from our food.

Chemists have learned the structure of vitamins and how they can be manufactured. Sometimes vitamins are added to foods to make up for those lost in processing. White flour and rice are usually artificially enriched in this way, because the vitamin-rich outer coatings of the grains have been removed in milling.

OTHER VITAL SUBSTANCES

A person can go for weeks without food and still survive, as long as he or she has water to drink. But cut out water, and the survival time drops to ten days or less.

Our bodies are about two-thirds water, which is as essential to life as any food. Many of the chemical processes of cells can take place only in a watery environment. Water in the tissues and in blood also carries food and oxygen to the cells and carries away wastes.

We lose part of our body water each day in our urine, bowel movements, and perspiration. To replace it, we need to drink plenty of fluids, even more in hot weather. Ordinarily the body signals when it needs water by making us feel thirsty.

THE MINERALS

If you have ever tasted perspiration, you know that body fluids are salty. The salty taste comes from the elements sodium and chlorine.

A major source for these elements is the mineral sodium chloride, which we know as table salt. When we perspire and lose other body fluid, we must replace the salt as well as the water. Ordinarily, we get more than enough salt from our daily diet.

Besides sodium and chlorine, the body needs small amounts of certain other elements. We get these from our food in the form of simple chemical compounds called *minerals*. Unlike the major food substances and vitamins, these minerals do not contain carbon as a key element.

Minerals are found in the water and soil around us. They are picked up by plants. The minerals then pass into the bodies of animals that eat the plants.

Our bodies need minerals that provide us with the elements calcium, cobalt, copper, iodine, iron, magnesium, phosphorus, potassium, sulfur, fluorine, and zinc. Each of these elements, though needed in small amounts, carries out one or more important jobs in the body.

Calcium, phosphorus, and fluorine go into bones and teeth to make them hard and strong. Magnesium helps bones and muscles do their jobs, and helps turn food into energy.

Besides sodium and chlorine from salt, the fluids in your body contain potassium. These minerals help keep the right amount of water inside cells.

Iron is found in the red blood cells. It helps those cells carry oxygen from the lungs to the rest of the body.

Iodine is needed to make a substance produced by the thyroid gland. This gland controls our growth.

Minerals often do several jobs. Zinc, for example, helps you grow, taste, make proteins, and heal wounds.

BOOSTING THE
MINERALS IN FOODS

Eating a wide variety of foods is the best way to insure you are getting enough of all the minerals. To help us get enough, extra amounts are sometimes put into our food. Iron is added to enriched white flour, for example, to replace that lost in milling. In Britain, chalk is added to bread to provide extra calcium. Many communities add fluorine to their drinking water to help strengthen teeth. A few years ago, American breakfast food manufacturers began adding extra vitamins and minerals to many cold cereals.

Lack of iodine used to be a problem in many communities where the soil was low in this element. Seafood is rich in iodine, but inland people often did not eat much seafood. This led to many cases of goiter, a disfiguring swelling of the neck caused by the enlargement of the thyroid gland. This health problem has been largely overcome by making *iodized salt* available in grocery stores.

Fresh fruits and vegetables are important
to a healthy diet, because they are
excellent sources of vitamins and minerals.

(41)

WHAT IS A GOOD DIET?

What have we discovered so far about what makes up a good diet? We have learned that we need fuel for body activities and material for growth. Carbohydrates and fats are good fuel sources. Proteins are the body builders.

To operate properly, the body needs small amounts of food substances called vitamins. We also need water, and minerals such as calcium and iron.

OUR BASIC DIET

In nations such as the United States, Canada, and Britain, there has been a shift in our "fuel foods." Today we eat fewer breadstuffs and more fats. This is partly a result of an increase in the consumption of meats and dairy foods.

Some medical scientists, though not all, believe there may be a link between our increased fat consumption and rising rates of heart disease. They are especially suspicious of animal fat, which is of the type known as "saturated" fat. The problem

(42)

here is that many other things affect the heart's health, such as smoking, lack of exercise, and obesity. It is not really clear just how much our fat intake has to do with heart disease.

To be on the safe side, many doctors recommend that we control our intake of animal fat. In some cases, "unsaturated" vegetable oils can be substituted. Vegetable oils can be used in cooking, for example, and margarine can be substituted for butter.

However, one way that families have cut back on animal fat is by eating fewer eggs and cutting down on milk and cheese. This deprives the family—especially growing children who need them the most—of valuable protein, minerals, and vitamins. Young people need dairy foods. Low-fat skim milk can be substituted for whole milk, if vitamins A and D are added to make up for the vitamins lost when the fat is removed.

OUR SWEET TOOTH

Nutritionists are also concerned that we are getting a larger share of carbohydrates in the form of sugar and sugary snacks and soft drinks.

People used to be content with fruits and small amounts of honey for sweets. They ate only a few pounds of table sugar per year. As sugar has become more plentiful and less expensive, our consumption has doubled and redoubled. Today, the average person consumes nearly 160 pounds a year. Much of this sugar is not eaten as table sugar but in pastries, candy, and soft drinks.

Two things about this rising use of sugar worry nutritionists. First, sugar provides "empty calories." Unlike orange juice, for example, a soft drink does not provide any vitamins or minerals. If we stave off hunger with sugary snacks or pop, we dull our appetites for more nutritious foods like fruits and vegetables.

Second, our love of sugar is blamed for much of our tooth decay. Sticky snack foods with particles that cling to our teeth and feed decay bacteria are the worst villains here.

DO WE GET
ENOUGH PROTEIN?

Besides the fuel foods, we need protein to build our bodies. Publicity about protein shortages in poor nations has led many people in our country to worry about getting enough protein. But surveys show that in general, families in the richer nations get plenty of protein. A survey made of American households in 1977–1978 by the U.S. Department of Agriculture found, for example, that lack of protein was not a problem even in most poor families.

OBESITY—
A WEIGHTY PROBLEM

Many people in the wealthier countries face a problem opposite to that of the populations of poorer countries. They take in more carbohydrate, fat, and protein than their bodies need. The extra food is stored as fat in the body, and the result is that people become overweight.

It's not so much that people are gluttons. It is simply that in our society, where we do a lot of sitting rather than physical work, we don't need the same amount of food that our farmer ancestors did. At the same time, the abundance of food, our snacking habits, and the custom of having food and drink at social gatherings encourage eating.

Scientists do not really know, however, the reasons why some people are able to satisfy their appetites without overeating while others cannot. Perhaps lack of exercise throws

(44)

the "appetite switch" out of whack so that it doesn't turn off when the overweight person has eaten enough. Perhaps some people turn to food to comfort themselves when they feel anxious or lonely.

Obesity brings both psychological and physical problems. In a society where we admire the slim and beautiful, over-weight people often feel ugly and out of place. In addition, they more often develop heart and blood system problems. Perhaps this is because their hearts and blood vessels have to work harder to move that extra weight around.

The end result is that dieting has become a part of the lives of millions of people. Dieting is hard because you have to change living habits built up over the years. You have to say "no" to yourself a lot, and it may take weeks or months for the "new, slim you" to emerge. This makes dieters prey to all sorts of trick diets that are described as "easy," "simple," "miraculous," and "instant."

If you want to diet, and many young people do, a doctor, dietician, or nutritionist can give you a sensible, healthy reducing plan that provides you with well-balanced nourishment while taking off weight gradually. The plan may include more exercise. If you stick to the plan, you will lose weight. Nature guarantees it.

VITAMINS
AND MINERALS

One important idea that you may have gotten from earlier chapters is that a narrow diet is a poor diet. Eating a wide variety of foods helps insure that you get enough of the necessary fuel, protein, vitamins, and minerals.

The discoverer of Vitamin A, Elmer McCollum, spent much of his life trying to get people to eat what he called *protective foods,* foods that have a rich supply of vitamins and minerals.

(45)

These protective foods are milk, vegetables, and fruits. In addition, certain foods have been artificially enriched with vitamins and minerals to help insure we get enough.

It is difficult for scientists to say exactly how much of each vitamin or mineral the body needs. This depends greatly upon the person's age, weight, sex, and eating habits. For example, we need more B vitamins if our diets are high in carbohydrates, because those vitamins help our bodies use carbohydrates.

Usually, the vitamin levels recommended by government health officials are a bit on the high side, just to be safe.

Surveys do show that some households are a bit low in their vitamin A and C intake. The vitamin A problem could be dealt with by eating more dairy foods and vegetables. An increase in our vegetable and fruit intake would take care of any possible vitamin C lack.

As for the minerals, only two seem to pose a problem. Some households don't get recommended levels of calcium, needed for strong bones and teeth. Calcium is especially needed by teen-agers. Here, more milk and cheese would be useful. Another mineral sometimes found in low supply is iron. Teen-age and adult women sometimes don't get enough iron to replace that lost in menstruation. This could be remedied by eating more iron-rich meats like liver, and more eggs.

Infants, pregnant women, and the elderly have special diet needs for which doctors may prescribe vitamins or mineral supplements. For most of us, pills are not needed. Massive doses of vitamins recommended by some, may be dangerous.

RATING YOUR
OWN DIET

How can we tell whether our own diet is balanced and nutritious? The DAILY FOOD GUIDE tells us what food groups it

DAILY FOOD GUIDE

FOOD GROUP	WHAT IT CONTAINS	WHY IMPORTANT	RECOM-MENDED SERVINGS EACH DAY
(1) Fruits and vegetables	Fruits include oranges, lemons, tangerines, grapefruit, apples, grapes, bananas, watermelon, cantaloupe, berries, etc. and their juices. Vegetables include peas, green beans, carrots, broccoli, corn, spinach, tomatoes, potatoes, etc.	These foods provide vitamins A and C, carbohydrates, and fiber. Each provides different amounts of these nutrients, so you should vary your selection each day. Fruits are particularly good for vitamin C, dark green and yellow vegetables for vitamin A.	4 (½ cup [120 ml] equals 1 serving.)
(2) Bread and cereals	All products made with whole grain or enriched flour, rice, or corn meal. These include bread, muffins, pancakes, breakfast cereals, rice, and enriched noodles and spaghetti.	This group gives your body some of the B vitamins and some iron. It is also a good source of carbo-hydrates. Whole grain bread and cereals also contain fiber and many important minerals that are not found in refined breads and cereals, not even artificially enriched ones.	4 Including some whole grain. (1 slice of bread equals 1 serving.)

(47)

DAILY FOOD GUIDE (continued)

FOOD GROUP	WHAT IT CONTAINS	WHY IMPORTANT	RECOMMENDED SERVINGS EACH DAY
(3) Milk and milk products	Whole, skim, or lowfat milk. Milk products such as cheese, yogurt, and cottage cheese.	These foods give you calcium and several vitamins, especially A and D. They also provide protein.	3 For children 10 and under 4 For older children and teenagers. (1 cup or 8-oz glass [240 ml] equals 1 serving.)
(4) Meat, poultry, fish, and beans	Chicken, fish, beef, veal, lamb, and pork. This group also includes eggs, cooked dried peas, beans, and lentils, nuts, and peanuts.	These foods provide protein, some B vitamins, and iron and zinc.	2 (About the same amount of meat as a medium hamburger patty equals 1 serving.)

DAILY FOOD GUIDE (*continued*)

FOOD GROUP	WHAT IT CONTAINS	WHY IMPORTANT	RECOM-MENDED SERVINGS EACH DAY
(5) Sugary and fatty foods	Sugary foods include sugar, honey, candy, chocolate, soft drinks, syrups, sweet toppings, jams, jellies, cookies, pastries, cakes, and pies. Fatty foods include butter and margarine, mayonnaise and other salad dressings, and fried snack-type foods such as potato chips.	Some items in this group provide a few vitamins and minerals, but mostly they just provide carbohydrates and fats, spoiling your appetite for more nutritious foods. You can get all the nourishment you need from the other food groups. Try to hold down your consumption of foods in this group.	You don't need a daily serving of any of these foods.

WORDS TO THE WISE

1. Some foods count for more than one group. Spaghetti with meat and tomato sauce, for example, scores for groups 1, 2, and 4.
2. If you don't like white milk, try stirring in a bit of chocolate to make it taste better to you. A couple of scoops of ice cream equal half a serving of milk, but don't try to substitute ice cream for a lot of your milk because it is rich in sugar and fat.
3. When we want a snack, we often pick foods from group 5. It's better to pick foods from the other four groups. Nutritious and satisfying snacks include fruit or fruit juice, carrot sticks and other raw vegetables, peanut butter sandwiches, nuts, pizza, raisins, and so forth.
4. Teen-age girls need a lot of iron. To help them get enough iron, they should eat plenty of iron-rich foods like liver, lean meat, shellfish, egg yolks, cooked dried beans or peas, green leafy vegetables, and whole-grain and enriched cereal products.

(49)

MARK	SHERYL
Breakfast	*Breakfast*
2 slices toast with jam	Egg
Orange juice	Slice of toast
	Grape juice
Lunch	*Lunch*
2 hamburgers with mustard	Tuna sandwich
Potato chips	Glass of chocolate milk
Cola drink	Salad
Afterschool Snack	*Afterschool Snack*
Pie	Piece of cheese pizza
Glass of milk	Celery sticks
Candy bar	
Dinner	*Dinner*
Roast beef	Chicken
Potatoes	Whole grain rice
Peas	Green beans
Glass of milk	Glass of milk
Evening Snack	*Evening Snack*
Several cookies	Peanuts
Cola drink	Cocoa

is wise to include in our daily diet, and how many servings of each group we need for healthful living. Of course, nobody's diet matches this one exactly, day after day. Some days we may get more milk than we need, some days less. What we need on the average is a good diet pattern.

At left are the foods Mark Edwards, age twelve, ate during one day. Next to them are the foods his neighbor, Sheryl Matthews, age ten, ate. Figure out how many servings of each food group each had during the day. Who had the more healthful diet—Mark or Sheryl?

Now that you've had some practice, keep track of your eating for the next two or three days. You may be surprised at what you find. Your food habits may not be what you think!

FOOD CONTROVERSIES

We are better nourished today than most people throughout history have ever been. Nutritional diseases that used to be common, such as rickets, are now rare. Each generation of children is taller than its parents. Surveys show that most households are getting the levels of vitamins and minerals recommended by researchers.

In spite of this, however, some people worry about our food and how it is grown, processed, and sold. We cannot discuss all these concerns in this brief book, but we can touch on a few of them.

A nurse from the World Health Organization teaches mothers in Niger how to make a nourishing cereal that will help their young children develop strong bodies.

(52)

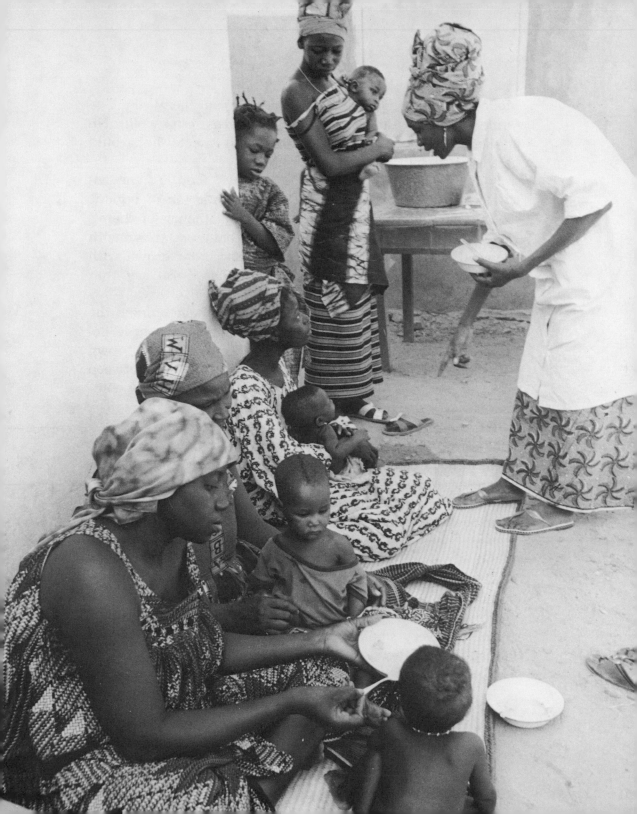

FOOD POLLUTION

Modern farming depends a great deal upon chemicals. The farmer applies fertilizers to the soil to increase crop yields. He applies pesticides to kill weeds, fungi, and insects that would destroy up to half his crop if not checked.

Some people argue in favor of "organic" food. To the scientist, all food is organic, but when people speak of organic food they usually mean food grown without the use of chemical fertilizers and pesticides. They argue that crops grown with chemical fertilizers are less nutritious than crops grown with manure and other "natural" fertilizers. They also say that traces of pesticides in our food are a serious health threat.

Most agricultural and food scientists who have studied the question say that there is little or no nutritive difference between foods grown with "chemical" fertilizers and those grown with "natural" ones. The plant sees no difference between nitrogen provided by manure and nitrogen provided by commercial fertilizer. It is the same element.

The question of pesticides is a little more complicated. Yes, some pesticides are very poisonous to people. We sometimes hear on the news about a farm worker killed by accidental exposure to a pesticide.

But the law requires that pesticides be used in ways that, when the crop is harvested, little or no pesticide is left on it.

LAW SETS LEVELS

Modern chemistry can detect incredibly small amounts of pesticides. Traces of pesticides are often found in foods in the grocery. However, the law requires that these traces, which are usually very small, be below a level considered safe for human consumption.

Scientists, however, must continue the search for better pesticides that will leave fewer traces in our food supplies.

Checks reveal that many of the "organic" foods sold in health food stores show the same levels of pesticides as those sold in the supermarket.

FOOD PROCESSING

Other critics find a great deal wrong with how our food is handled between farm and table.

A common argument is that commercial food processing, such as canning, freezing, and milling, destroys much of the healthfulness of our food.

This is simply not true in most cases. Modern food processing, by and large, simply does on a large scale what a cook does at home in the kitchen. Nutrients are lost in commercial food processing such as canning, but often the loss is smaller than occurs in home cooking. What loss does occur makes little practical difference in the average diet. Where there is a serious loss of vitamins and minerals, as in the milling of white flour, the loss is made up by adding back the most important missing nutrients.

WHAT ABOUT ADDITIVES?

The food industry makes use of many different substances in processing foods. These substances are known as *additives*.

Some additives are put in food to improve the flavor. Salt and sugar are common additives. Another one is monosodium glutamate, or MSG.

Other additives are put in foods to keep them fresh between the time the food leaves the factory and the time it is

used to feed someone. Bakers, for example, often add calcium propionate or sodium propionate to prevent the growth of mold on baked goods. Ascorbic acid (vitamin C) is often added to frozen fruits and vegetables to prevent color changes and other deterioration.

Some additives make food more attractive to the consumer. For example, margarine is colored yellow to make it resemble butter; otherwise it would be an unappetizing white.

The food industry makes use of thousands of additives, most of them substances found in plants or animals naturally. MSG, for example, was first used long ago by Asians in the form of dried seaweed. Like MSG, salt, and the spices, many additives have been used in cooking for centuries.

Some additives, particularly certain food dyes, are products of chemical research. They were first made in the laboratory.

Because it was shown that several additives, including one dye, might be harmful to human health, laws concerning these substances have been tightened in recent years. New additives must pass safety tests before being used by the food industry. Traditional additives are being tested for safety while they are still permitted to be used.

Here, as with pesticides, absolute safety cannot be guaranteed. On the other hand, most food scientists believe that the additives now being used in our food are very safe in the amounts added. Without them, a great deal of our food would be lost to spoilage. Some foods such as ice cream would not

*Bread baked in an automated bakery
often contains additives to keep it fresh
on the grocer's shelf or to replace
nutrients that are lost in processing.*

even be available commercially, because without additives they would not stand up to storage and transportation.

Certainly, we should be careful in our selection of foods. But our shopping should be based on facts and our own tastes, not on fear or fads. The ordinary grocery or supermarket provides all we need for an adequate diet. If we want our foods fresher and without "chemicals," by all means let us plant gardens. But we do not have to buy expensive vitamin supplements, "organic" foods, or "health" foods to enjoy good nutrition.

GLOSSARY

Additive: any substance added in small amounts to food during processing.

Amino acid: one of the basic chemical building blocks from which proteins are constructed. *Essential amino acids* are those the body cannot manufacture but must get from food.

Beriberi: a disease caused by lack of vitamin B_1, or thiamine, which leads to partial paralysis of the limbs.

Calorie: a unit of measure for heat. The calorie unit used in nutrition is the large calorie, sometimes capitalized, which is equal to 1,000 calories.

Carbohydrate: sugar, starch, cellulose, and certain other substances that are built from sugar molecules.

Carbon: the organic element that is the basis of life.

Carbon dioxide: gas formed by the union of carbon and oxygen.

Cellulose: the fibrous or woody substance in plants.

Enzyme: a substance that triggers a chemical change but is not used up in the process.

Fatty acid: one of the basic chemical building blocks from which fats and oils are constructed. An *essential fatty acid* is one necessary for good health.

Fiber: the plant material that passes undigested through the stomach and small intestine; also called roughage.

Iodized salt: table salt to which iodine has been added.

Mineral: element or compound that the body needs, usually in small amounts, for good health. Unlike other food substances, minerals do not contain carbon.

Molecule: the smallest particle into which a substance can be divided without changing the nature of the substance. Molecules are made up of one or more atoms.

Nutrition: the nourishment of the body; also, the scientific study of how we are nourished.

Obesity: the condition of being overweight, especially greatly overweight.

Protective foods: foods such as milk, vegetables, and fruits that help insure one gets enough vitamins and minerals.

Protein: long-chain molecules containing nitrogen, and essential to life.

Rickets: disease in which bones are poorly formed due to lack of calcium or lack of vitamin D.

Roughage: fibers and other plant substances not absorbed by intestines but which help provide bulk to feces.

Scurvy: disease caused by lack of vitamin C, in which gums become spongy and bleed; there is bleeding under the skin, and the victim becomes weak.

Starch: food substance made up of chains of sugar molecules.

Vitamin: plant or animal substance needed in small amounts for good health.

FOR FURTHER READING

Berger, Melvin and Gilda. *The New Food Book*. New York: Thomas Y. Crowell, 1978.

Cameron, Allan G. *Food—Facts and Fallacies*. London: Faber and Faber, 1971.

Deutsch, Ronald M. *The New Nuts Among the Berries: How Nutrition Nonsense Captured America*. Palo Alto, CA.: Bull Publishing, 1977.

Elgin, Kathleen. *The Human Body: The Digestive System*. New York: Franklin Watts, Inc., 1973.

Goldman, M. C. and Hylton, William H., eds. *The Basic Book of Organically Grown Foods*. Emmaus, PA.: Rodale Press, 1972.

Pyke, Magnus, *Man and Food*. New York-Toronto: McGraw-Hill, 1970.

Tannenbaum, Beulah and Stillman, Myra. *Understanding Food: The Chemistry of Nutrition*. New York-Toronto: McGraw-Hill, 1962.

U.S. Department of Agriculture. *What's to Eat? and Other Questions Kids Ask About Foods*. Washington, D.C.: Office of Superintendent of Documents, 1979.

Wilson, Wendy and Jacobson, Michael. *Food Scorecard*. Washington, D.C.: Center for Science In the Public Interest, 1974.

Woolfolk, Dorothy A. *The Teenage Surefire Diet Cookbook*. New York: Franklin Watts, Inc., 1979.

Zim, Herbert S. *Your Stomach and Digestive Tract*. New York: William Morrow, 1973.

INDEX

(64)

Oxygen, 12, 14, 24, 27; experiment with, 15

Pepsin, 31
Pesticides, 7, 54, 57
Phosphorus, 39
Population, 2, 6–7, 10
Potassium, 39
Proteins, 12, 24, 27, 30–31, 33, 42, 44; sources of, 32

Rice, 35
Rickets, 36, 52
Root vegetables, 22
Roughage, 25

Saliva, 22
Salivary amylase, 22, 24
Salt, in body, 38–39; as additive, 55, 57
Saturated fat, 42
Scavenging, 2
Scurvy, 18, 35
Smoking, 43
Snacking, 21, 28–29, 43, 49
Sodium, 38–39
Sodium chloride, 39
Sodium propionate, 57
Spices, 57
Spoilage, 57
Starch, 22; chain, 24
Starchy foods, 31
Stark, William, 18
Starvation, 34
Stomach, 24

Storing fuel, 26
Sugar, 12, 20–22, 24; as additive, 55: snacks, 43
Sugary and fatty foods, chart, 49
Sulfur, 39

Tendons, 13
Thyroid gland, 41
Tissue, 11
Tools, 6
Tooth decay, 21, 44

Unsaturated fat, 43
Upper digestive tract, 27
Urban nations, 7

Vegetable oils, 26
Vegetarians, 33
Vitamins, 21, 36–37, 39, 42, 46; B vitamins, 22, 37, 46; vitamin A, 36–37, 43, 45–46; vitamin C, 18, 46, 57; vitamin D, 43, 46

Wars, 6
Waste heat, 17
Wasting away, 30
Water, 12–13, 38, 42
Weapons, 2, 6
Weight problems, 29. See also obesity
World Health Organization, 53
World population, 2, 6–7, 10

Zinc, 39